GW00498401

For You Mum

For You Mum

A Heartwarmers™ Gift Book

WPL

For You Mum

A Heartwarmers™ Gift Book

©WPL 2002

Text by A. Fisher

Additional material by Howard Baker

Illustration by Dolen Corbridge - Advocate

Printed in China

Published by WPL 2002

ISBN 1-904264-04-2

For information on other Heartwarmers™ gift books,
gifts and greetings cards, please contact

WPL

14 Victoria Ind. Est. Wales Farm Road

London W3 6UU UK

Tel: +44 (0) 208 993 7268 Fax: +44 (0) 208 993 8041

email: wpl@atlas.co.uk

Mum, I just wanted you to know
of my appreciation,
for all the years of love and care,
your time and dedication.

I have so much to thank you for,
love and kindness to repay,
and I hope this little book conveys
all the things I want to say.

Every Mum is special
of that there is no doubt,
but you are the very best
- that's what I want to shout !

You have so many qualities
you're practical and smart,
but best of all I think is that
you have the biggest heart.

Thanks for the
sacrifices you've made,
for your selfless
devotion and care,
for the endless patience
you've had and for
always being there.

Growing up isn't easy
but I hope you've always known,
how much I really love you
even if it hasn't shown.

As a child when there were times
that I felt afraid,
you would always be there
and come straight to my aid.

Having a Mum
like you around
to encourage and reassure,
made me feel like I was safe,
protected and secure.

You set me a good example
steadfast, loyal and strong,
and taught me the difference
between what's right
and what is wrong.

You gave me the confidence
that every young person needs,
to leave the nest,
explore the world,
and follow
where life leads.

Mum, I know I have my faults
just like all the rest,
and yet you always make me feel
I'm up there with the best.

Even when I do something
that would make others frown,
you keep your sense of humour
and you never put me down.

You have always made me feel
like I'm top of your agenda,
and the love you've given me
has always been so tender.

You tell me I'm so special
no matter what I do.
I know I'm so very lucky
to have a Mum like you.

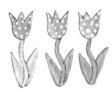

Whenever things
don't go as planned
you've always encouraged me,
to simply try and try again
to be the best that I can be.

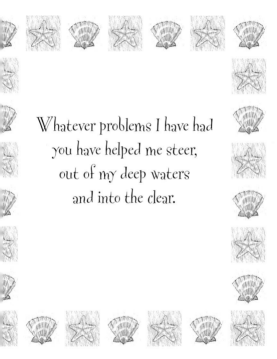

Whatever problems I have had
you have helped me steer,
out of my deep waters
and into the clear.

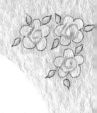

I'm so happy to have a Mum
I can talk to when I'm blue,
and life would not be half as nice
if I did not have you.

Some people are special
but you, Mum, are unique,
and you can always cheer me up
when things are looking bleak.

You've raised my spirits often
when I have felt depressed,
supported and encouraged me
when life has got me stressed.

You can see when I'm in trouble
even when I can't,
and you give me really good advice
like the best Agony Aunt.

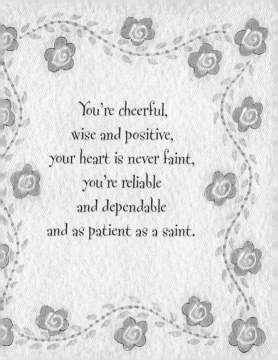

You're cheerful,
wise and positive,
your heart is never faint,
you're reliable
and dependable
and as patient as a saint.

I'm so grateful that I have
a Mum who understands,
who is always there to help me
to realise my plans.

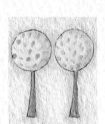

Mum, I think you really are
worth your weight in gold.
Your humour and your wisdom
are a wonder to behold.

You look on the bright side
whenever things get rough,
and are incredibly supportive
when life seems so tough.

You're such a special person
with qualities so rare,
compassion, understanding,
and a warmth beyond compare.

You've always
been someone
on whom I can depend,
but as well as being
a brilliant Mum
you've also been
my friend.

All the happy
times we've had
are moments
that I treasure,
and the love I feel
inside for you
is impossible to measure.

Mum, I want to return to you
all the kindness you have shown,
as you're the nicest person
I have ever known.

You're full of optimism,
generosity and grace,
and if everyone had a Mum like you
the world would be a happier place.

I will always cherish
the special bond we share,
and even when we are apart
we know it's always there.

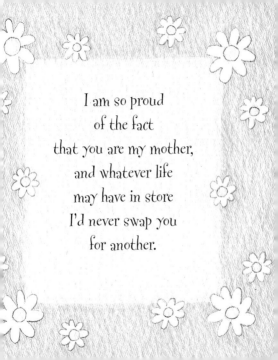

I am so proud
of the fact
that you are my mother,
and whatever life
may have in store
I'd never swap you
for another.

In return for all your love
which I hold so dear,
I want you to know
that for you, Mum,
I'll always be here.

I want you to remember, Mum,
wherever you go
and whatever you do,
wherever life may take us
I'll always love you.

I Love You Mum

A Heartwarmers™
Gift Book

WPL

Also available from Heartwarmers

Thank you Mum

For a Special Friend

For my Sister

100 Reasons why I Love You

For my Husband

To a Good Friend

Believe in Yourself

For my Nan

I Love You Because...

For a Special Daughter

For a Special Mum